Another Great Achiever

Helen Keller

Facing Her Challenges
Challenging the World

By Janet and Geoff Benge
Illustrated by Kennon James

Advance PUBLISHING, INC • HOUSTON

Permissions
Advance Publishing, Inc.
6950 Fulton St.
Houston, TX 77022

www.advancepublishing.com

First Edition
Printed in Singapore

Library of Congress Cataloging-in-Publication Data

Benge, Janet, 1958-
   Helen Keller: Facing Her Challenges, Challenging the World / by Janet and Geoff Benge: illustrated by Kennon James.
      p. cm. -- (Another Great Achiever)
   Summary: The life of the woman who graduated from college with honors and traveled around the world on behalf of the physically handicapped even though she had been blind and deaf since early childhood.
      ISBN 1-57537-107-3 (hardcover: alk. paper). -- ISBN 1-57537-105-7 (library binding: alk. paper)
   1. Keller, helen, 1880-1968 Juvenile literature. 2. Blind-deaf women--United States Biography Juvenile literature.   3. Blind-deaf--United States Biography Juvenile literature. 4. Sullivan, Annie, 1866-1936 Juvenile literature. [Keller, Helen, 1880-1968. 2. Blind. 3. Deaf. 4. Physically handicapped. 5. Women Biography. 6. Sullivan, Annie, 1866-1936.] I. Benge, Geoff, 1954- II. James, Kennon, ill. III. Title. IV. Series.
HV1624.K4B423 2000
362.4'1'092--dc21   99-33410
[B]   CIP

Another Great Achiever

Helen Keller

Facing Her Challenges
Challenging the World

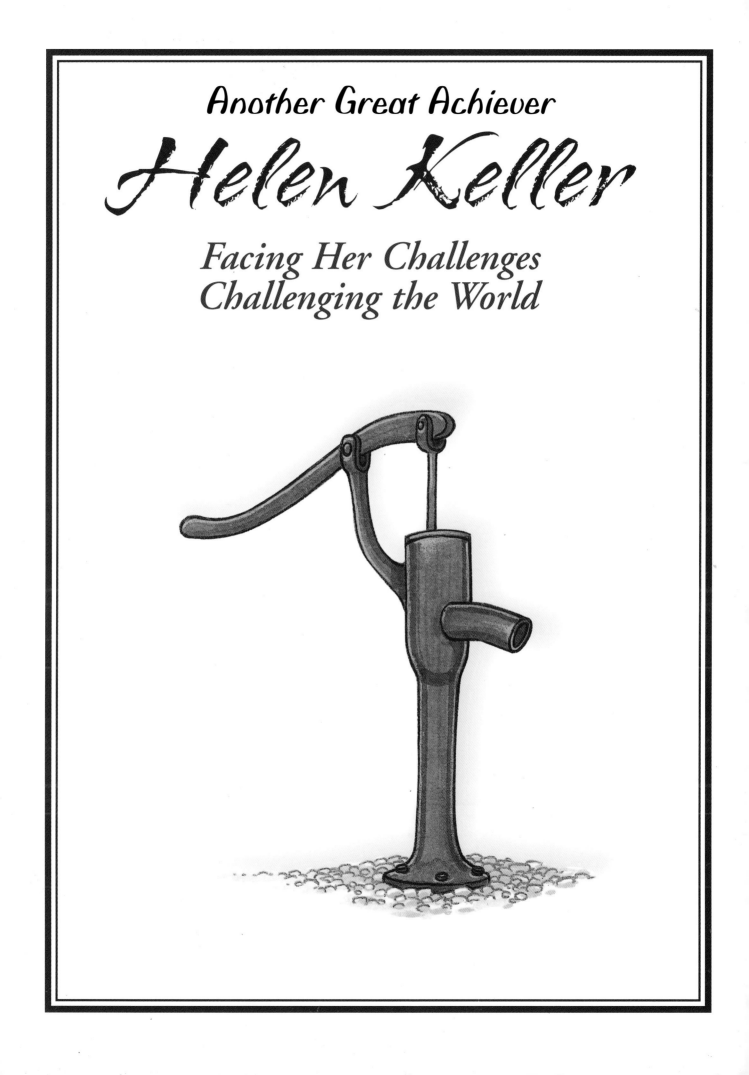

4

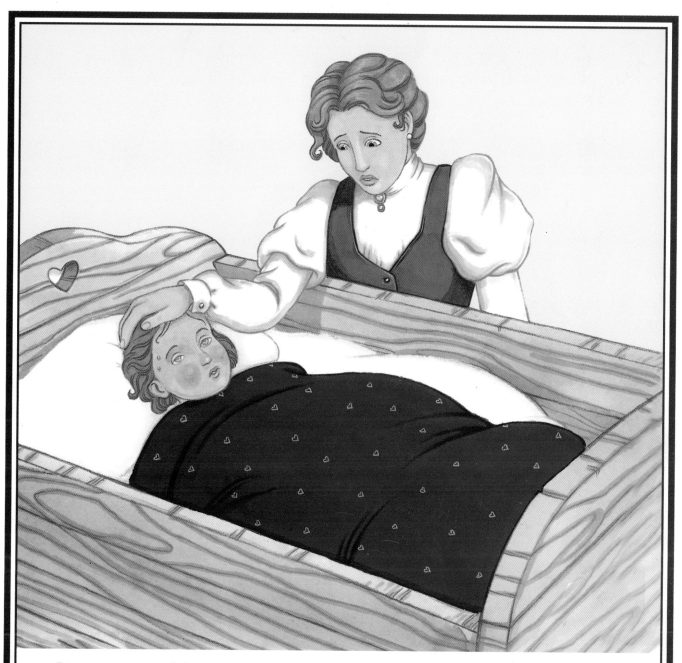

It was a cold, crisp morning in Alabama. The year was 1882, and one-year-old Helen Keller couldn't seem to wake up properly. She heard her mother and father whispering above her crib. She felt a hand on her forehead, and heard footsteps across the floor.

Helen lay in her crib, too sick to know what was happening to her. She was burning up with fever. Sometimes she could hear her mother singing to her, but the voice seemed to be getting further and further away. Little Helen did not know it, but she had scarlet fever.

The doctor came to see her every day, but there was little he could do. There was no cure for scarlet fever. He'd seen many adults die from the illness, and he was sure there was no hope for a small child like Helen. He felt very sorry for Captain and Mrs. Keller. Their only child, who they loved very much, was going to die. Yet no matter what the doctor said, the Kellers would not give up hope. Over and over they reminded themselves that Helen was strong-willed, even stubborn—too stubborn to die. And they were right.

Bit by bit, Helen began to get better. Her parents, grandparents, aunts, uncles, even the servants were excited at her progress. They told each other that in no time at all little Helen would be running around the house, laughing and playing silly tricks just like she used to. What they did not know was that something terrible had happened to Helen while she was sick. The scarlet fever had damaged her body—and that damage could never be undone.

Before she had become sick, Helen had five senses—five ways to find out about the world around her. She could see, hear, smell, feel and taste things. But now, as she recovered from scarlet fever, two of those senses were missing. Sure, Helen got well again, but she could no longer see or hear. She was destined to live in a world of darkness and silence.

Being so young, Helen could not understand what had happened to her. She could feel it when her mother lifted her up and sponged her body with a wet cloth. But why didn't her mother talk to her? And she could feel the wind when her father opened the door, and the vibrations of his footsteps on the floor. But why did he always visit her in the dark? Helen lay in her crib, waiting for things to be the same as they were before—but nothing changed.

Captain and Mrs. Keller were heart broken; their bright and happy little girl was now deaf and blind. The house no longer rang with her laughter, and there was no sound of little feet as she trotted down the hallway in search of adventure. Now all Helen did was cling to her mother's skirt all day. She was terrified of being left alone.

The Kellers had enough money to try everything that might help Helen. They wanted her to see and hear again, so they took her to special doctors. But none of the doctors could help. It was hopeless. In time Captain and Mrs. Keller understood that Helen would never see or hear again.

By the time she was five, Helen had become very angry. Her parents didn't know what to do. They felt sorry for her and let her do whatever she wanted. At meal times she felt her way around the table, grabbing food from other people's plates. She would stuff her mouth full and throw food around, but her mother couldn't bring herself to tell Helen to behave. She felt it would be unfair to expect someone who was blind and deaf to have good manners.

Even after deliberately locking her mother in the pantry for half a day, Helen wasn't punished. And the older Helen got, the more difficult she became. Some people thought Helen should be sent to a hospital for insane people. But Captain and Mrs. Keller wanted to keep Helen at home with them as long as they could. Nobody thought Helen should go to school. What would be the use? How could a person who was deaf and blind learn anything? How could she communicate with anyone?

One person, however, noticed that Helen was smart. Aunt Evelina had watched her closely, counting the number of signs Helen had invented to communicate with others. There were over sixty of them. Helen let the cook know she wanted a sandwich by pretending to cut a slice of bread. She asked for ice cream by shivering. Helen even had signs for the names of her parents. For her mother, she put her hair up in a bun; for her father she acted as if she were putting on glasses. When she pretended to tie a bonnet under her chin, her parents knew that Helen wanted to visit her aunt.

Aunt Evelina worried about Helen. She felt sure Helen didn't belong in a hospital with insane people. But what would happen to Helen when she grew up?

All the while lots of thoughts and feelings were going on inside Helen; but she had no way to tell anyone about them—no way to ask questions. And she had many questions to ask. Why did her father put a wire and glass thing on his face and hold up sheets of paper every night after dinner? And why did her mother keep changing the threads on her sewing machine, when all the threads felt identical? What Helen had no way of knowing, of course, was that her father owned a newspaper, and after dinner each night he'd put on his glasses and read the latest edition of the paper from cover to cover. Nor could she know that her mother was sewing a dress that needed many different colored threads. Or that the new dress was for the new Keller baby.

With the baby growing inside her mother, Helen eventually noticed she could no longer sit in her mother's lap. She was five when her sister, Mildred, was born. Helen was happy thinking she would finally get her mother back all to herself. Of course, that didn't happen. Baby Mildred took up most of her mother's time. Helen began to hate her new sister.

One day when she was alone with Mildred, she tipped her out of her crib. Fortunately, Mildred wasn't hurt; but her parents were shocked.

Perhaps people were right after all—Helen should be sent away to the hospital before she really hurt someone with her temper tantrums. Yet something inside the Kellers wouldn't give up. There had to be a way to help Helen.

One day, Mrs. Keller read about Alexander Graham Bell who had just invented the telephone. She read that both Mr. Bell's mother and wife were deaf, and that he had invented some wonderful ways to help them. Perhaps he could help Helen.

Soon Captain Keller and six-year-old Helen were on a train headed for Washington, D.C. to visit Alexander Graham Bell. Helen was very excited. She could feel the vibrations of the train as it rumbled along the track. And she breathed in the hot steam as it billowed from the engine.

When they got to Washington, Captain Keller and Alexander Graham Bell talked for a long time. Helen sat on Mr Bell's knee and played with his pocket watch, holding it against her cheek so she could feel it tick. Mr. Bell told Helen's father about a woman named Laura Bridgman. She was blind and deaf too. She lived in Boston at the Perkins Institute for the Blind, where she had been taught to read and write. Mr. Bell said Captain Keller should write to the Perkins Institute to see if they could help Helen.

As soon as they got home to Alabama, Captain Keller wrote to the Perkins Institute. The director wrote back saying that Helen should have a private tutor, and he knew just the person for the job—Annie Sullivan. Annie was twenty-years-old and had just graduated from the Institute. She could live with Helen and be her teacher. The Kellers weren't very enthusiastic about the plan. The director had also written that Annie Sullivan had gone blind when she was five-years-old and had spent most of her childhood in a poorhouse with hundreds of drunk, crippled, and insane people. When she was fourteen a kind man met her and paid for her to go to the Perkins Institute. While at Perkins, Annie had eye surgery and was now able to see fairly well. The Kellers wondered how someone with Annie's background could possibly be a good influence on Helen. What they didn't know was that Annie was every bit as stubborn as Helen, and that they would make a perfect pair.

After much discussion, the Kellers finally decided they had no choice. Annie Sullivan would be better than no one, so they invited her to live with them.

Annie's eyes grew wide when she met Helen. The six-year-old girl in front of her was more animal than human. Her hair had not been combed for weeks—she wouldn't let her mother near it. Her body was filthy—she didn't like baths, and her shoe laces were untied—she kicked anyone who tried to tie them. Annie was also shocked at Helen's table manners. She grabbed food, threw it on the floor, and spat out what she didn't like. All the while, Captain and Mrs. Keller smiled, telling Annie that Helen didn't understand about manners.

Annie disagreed. She thought Helen could understand what she wanted to understand. What Helen needed was to learn to obey. She knew it would be impossible to teach Helen anything until she could get her to sit still and concentrate.

Annie wrote to a friend about Helen, saying, "The greatest problem I have to solve is how to discipline and control her without breaking her spirit.... It [is] useless to try to teach her language or anything else until she [learns] to obey me.... Obedience is the gateway through which knowledge... and love... enter the mind of a child."

For many weeks the Keller house was not a happy place. Annie and Helen were in a battle, and the Kellers were on Helen's side. Many times Captain Keller told Annie she was being too harsh. He couldn't stand to see his little girl cry. Of course she was doing more than crying—she was pinching and hitting and kicking anyone who didn't give her what she wanted, when she wanted it. One day Helen went into a rage and knocked out Annie's two front teeth. But Annie would not give in. She knew that once Helen realized she was there to help her, Helen would use all of that stubbornness to learn.

One morning at breakfast, Annie had seen enough. Helen was snatching food from people's plates. When she reached over to Annie's plate, Annie slapped her hand. Helen was shocked! So she reached over again. Again Annie slapped her hand. And so it went on: Reach, slap, reach slap.

Captain and Mrs. Keller didn't know what to say, so they left the dining room. Annie locked the door firmly behind them. The battle of wills had begun. Helen kicked and pinched, sulked and pouted, but there was no way she could get the food off Annie's plate. Annie slapped her hand every time she tried. After several hours, Helen finally gave in and ate the food on her own plate. But the battle began all over again when Annie motioned for Helen to fold her napkin. Another hour went by, and it was lunch time before they were done with breakfast. Annie was exhausted, but she was excited too. Something wonderful had happened. Helen had obeyed for the first time.

Annie knew she had to be left alone with Helen so she would learn to obey more. The Keller's weren't very happy about leaving their little girl alone with Annie; after all, she might cry again. But in the end they agreed to let Annie and Helen move into a little cottage in the garden. In the cottage Annie made up the rules. Helen did not get food unless she used a spoon and a napkin, and she did not go outside until she was properly washed and dressed with her shoe laces tied. Soon, Helen knew she had lost the battle. She would have to obey Annie to get what she wanted.

Within a week, Helen was ready to learn to spell. Over and over, Annie would make the shape of letters and words on Helen's hand. Helen would copy this "hand-talking," but she had no idea what words were, or why she was learning these shapes with her teacher.

One day, Helen became very angry and smashed her china doll. She was tired of learning shapes that had no meaning. Annie decided they should take a walk in the garden. The scent of the flowers and the touch of the rustling leaves always soothed Helen. Together they walked to the water pump. Annie got Helen to hold a mug under the spout while she pumped. Water quickly filled the mug and overflowed onto Helen's hand. Meanwhile, Annie spelled "w-a-t-e-r" in Helen's other hand—slowly at first, then faster and faster.

Helen seemed startled. She dropped the mug and stood still. Somewhere inside her head a connection was being made. The cool, wet liquid flowing over one hand had a shape, the shape Annie was spelling out in her other hand. In a joyful moment, Helen understood. Everything had a matching shape—and that shape was it's name!

Helen was wild with excitement, she ran around the garden touching the flowers, the fence, the grass, the dirt. Annie knew what she wanted to know. Quickly she hand-talked the name of each thing on Helen's hand. Next Helen touched Annie. Annie spelled back "T-e-a-c-h-e-r". Then Helen touched herself, and Annie spelled out "H-e-l-e-n K-e-l-l-e-r". For the first time in her life, Helen knew she had a name. She kept on touching things until she was completely drained of energy. By the time she went to bed that night, she had learned thirty new words—and this time it all made sense.

What a wonderful day! Helen "talked" to herself until her fingers were too tired to move. She was so excited, for her mind understood things like never before—as did her heart. She realized that all the things Annie had done for her were because she cared—even the spankings!

That night for the first time, Helen of her own accord snuggled into bed with Annie and gave her a kiss. Later, Annie wrote, "I thought my heart would burst, it was so full of joy."

Helen was a fast learner. Within three months she could spell over three hundred words, and she was able to use them in little sentences which she hand-talked to Annie.

Annie taught Helen all kinds of things. But to really learn about something, Helen liked to feel it. Animals particularly fascinated her. One day Annie took an egg which was just about to hatch and placed it in Helen's hand. Helen felt the egg vibrate. Then she felt a sharp little beak poke out. The chick was pecking its way out of the egg right in Helen's hand! Helen was delighted. Not long after this, Annie showed Helen a small pig and Helen asked if she could feel the shell the piglet had pecked through. Annie explained that not every baby animal came out of an egg.

Annie Sullivan had some very unusual ways of teaching Helen. A lot of people did not understand and criticized her. But Annie knew what she was doing and was determined Helen should learn the way that was the most meaningful for her. Helen loved to sit in trees where she could feel the branches sway in the breeze and smell the flowers below. Sometimes insects even landed on her, and very lightly Helen would feel their delicate shape. Every day, Annie would hitch up her long skirt and climb into a tree with Helen. Together, high up in the branches they would have school.

At other times, Annie would lead Helen down to the bank of a stream and make the shapes of countries in the mud. Helen would feel the shape and ask questions about the world. Helen learned how streams run into rivers, the whereabouts of mountain ranges, and how countries fit together.

On the way home, they would walk through the woods. Whenever Annie saw a dead animal, she would guide Helen over to it, letting her feel its fur and the muscles and bones underneath.

Climbing trees, coming home wet and muddy, feeling dead animals, it was all very odd to Helen's family. But Helen was learning, and they were grateful for that. So they left Annie and Helen to do as they pleased. In fact, by Christmas that year the Kellers were more than thrilled with Annie's labor. Mrs. Keller exclaimed to Annie, "I thank God every day for sending you to us." Captain Keller took Annie's hand but was speechless.

Within a few months of Annie's arrival, Helen had also learned to read Braille books. In these books, the letters were made up of raised dots. Helen read them by feeling across the dots with her fingers. Helen also learned to write normally with a pencil. She would place a piece of paper over a board that looked much like a checker board. The board had deep squares cut into it, and Helen learned to write the shape of each letter inside a square. She used her left hand to guide her right hand across the page. This was called "square-hand script," and Helen got quite good at writing it. The only problem was that she had no way of reading back what she'd written because the words were flat on the page.

One day, when Helen was seven years old, Annie took her to the circus. There she shook hands with a bear and was licked by a leopard. She was also lifted up so she could feel a giraffe's neck, and she followed the circus performers around the ring. Helen was even invited up on stage where a monkey stole her hat. Everyone laughed, but Helen laughed most of all. At last she was beginning to understand and enjoy the wonderful world around her.

The following May, when Helen was eight years old, an even bigger adventure awaited her. The director of the Perkins Institute for the Blind invited Helen, her mother, and Annie to come to Boston. Helen enjoyed every minute of her visit. She loved riding the train and the bustle of the big city. But most of all, she enjoyed the friendship of other children her own age. All the children at the Perkins Institute could hand-talk, and for the first time in her life, Helen could talk directly to someone other than Annie. She wanted to learn all about her new friends. And they wanted to learn about Helen.

Other people were also interested in Helen. Helen didn't know it, but she had become famous all over the world. Many newspaper articles had been written about her. Even President Cleveland invited her to the White House to visit him.

Annie realized it was important for Helen to talk to lots of different types of people. So she invited many people to visit them. As the person spoke, Annie would hand-talk to Helen what they were saying, and then she would repeat what Helen was hand-talking back.

Bishop Brooks, the local minister, was one person who spent a lot of time with Helen in Boston. They became good friends. Helen enjoyed the many hours they spent together "talking" about God and love and goodness.

While Helen had a wonderful time in Boston, she was glad to go home, too. There was so much to do. Her dog, Lioness, was waiting for her, as was her horse, Black Beauty, which she loved to ride. And Helen had a lot of thank-you letters to write to people back in Boston. To Bishop Brooks she wrote, "It fills my heart with joy to know that God loves me so much that he wishes me to live always, and that he gives me everything that makes me happy, loving friends, a precious little sister, sweet flowers, and best of all, a heart that can love and sympathize and a mind that can think and enjoy. I am thankful to my heavenly father for giving me all these precious things."

Every winter for the next four years, Annie took Helen back to the Perkins Institute where she learned many things. She was taught pottery and physical education. She even learned French and Greek, spending countless hours in the library. The Perkins Institute had the largest collection of Braille books in the world. There was only one problem with these books for the blind—they used five different raised dot alphabets to write the words. Helen wanted to read all the books, so she had to learn all five alphabets. This seemed very unfair for blind people, and Helen promised herself that one day she would do something about it.

When Helen was ten years old, a friend wrote to her about Tommy Stringer. He was a five-year-old blind and deaf boy who was living in a poorhouse in Pennsylvania. Helen decided to help Tommy. She wrote to everyone she could think of—friends, relatives, even newspapers, asking for money to send Tommy to the Perkins Institute. Much to Helen's surprise, the money poured in. It was enough to pay for all of Tommy's schooling. For the first time, Helen felt the joy of helping someone else. She determined to spend the rest of her life helping others.

Helen liked to be outdoors most of all. She could feel the sun and the wind, the rain and the fog, and smell nature all around her. Helen, her mother, and Annie often made trips together. One visit they made was to Niagara Falls. Helen loved it there. She could feel the thundering vibrations of the mighty falls and the water spraying in her face.

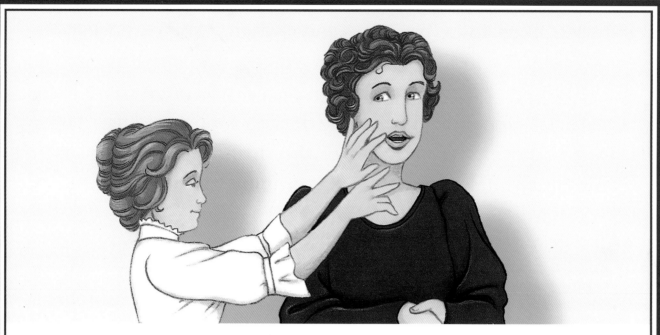

At 14 years old, Helen enrolled at the Wright-Humason School in New York City. She and Annie lived there for the next two years. At the Wright-Humason School, Helen learned to lip-read. A deaf person learns to lip-read by watching the way a speaker's lips and face move when talking. Of course, Helen couldn't see the speaker, so she had to learn a different way. Once again Helen used her hands. She felt the vibrations of the speaker's throat and the way the lips and tongue moved. At the same time, she felt how the air was going in and out of the speaker's mouth. This was very difficult, and Helen had to practice for a long time. But she did not give up until she learned.

Helen also wanted to learn to talk. Because she couldn't hear what she was saying or look in the mirror at the shapes her lips made, this was even harder than learning to lip-read. Although she practiced and practiced speaking, few people could understand her. Sometimes she spoke too loudly, other times she spoke too softly, and she did not stop and start at the right places to make sentences. But she never gave up trying, and over the years her speech got better and better.

While Helen was at the Wright-Humason School, she had a big idea. She decided she would go to a traditional college and learn alongside hearing and seeing students. She set her sights on Radcliffe College, the top university for women in the United States. It was hard to pass the entrance exam for Radcliffe, even for the hearing and seeing. Many people said it would be impossible for Helen. And even if she did pass, college might make her brain work too hard and give her brain damage! They tried to get Annie to change Helen's mind, but Annie wouldn't even try. She knew that once Helen had made up her mind, there was no stopping her!

When she was 19 years old, Helen Keller passed the entrance exam and entered Radcliffe College! But school officials told her they couldn't make many special arrangements for her. Either she would find a way to keep up with the other students or she would fail.

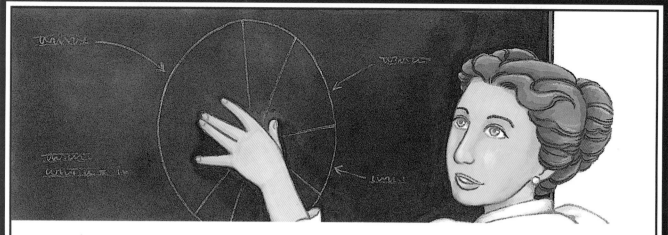

Helen and Annie went to work. They sat side by side in lectures where Annie spelled each word the teacher said into Helen's hand. (They could hand-talk at 80 words per minute, almost as fast as people normally speak.) Sometimes, to help her understand diagrams the teacher had drawn, Helen would run her fingers over the chalkboard. Her fingers were so sensitive she could feel the chalk lines and "see" the diagrams.

After class, Helen would rush back to her room and type out on a Braille typewriter everything she could remember about the lecture. Using a Braille typewriter meant she could read the notes back with her fingers to study for tests. To take a test, Helen had the questions hand-talked to her by a college official. Helen then typed her answers on a regular typewriter so the teacher could read and grade them. Of course, Helen couldn't read back what she had typed, so it was fortunate she had a good memory.

While attending Radcliffe College, Helen learned to read and write French, German, Greek, and Latin. She even served as class vice president. People were amazed the day it actually happened—the day Helen Keller, blind and deaf, graduated with honors from one of the top colleges in the world!

How had she done it? People wanted to know. To answer their questions, Helen wrote a book called, *The Story of My Life*. A man named John Macy edited the book. Thousands of Americans read the book and came to understand what Helen Keller had been communicating all along: Given a chance, the physically challenged can do all manner of things. People in other countries wanted to know all about Helen, too. Before long, her book was translated into 50 languages.

Years later President Woodrow Wilson asked her why she chose Radcliffe when she could have entered an easier college. "Because they didn't want me at Radcliffe," she said, "and being stubborn, I chose to override their objections."

Helen was happy. People were beginning to understand that those who were blind, deaf, and lame were not useless. She began to write more and more. She wrote articles on how to stop blindness and on how the seeing-impaired should do as much for themselves as possible.

Again, John Macy edited her work, and he, Helen, and Annie became a writing team. Helen began to think that Annie and John were falling in love, and she was right. In 1905 they were married. John moved into the house with Annie and Helen. Annie continued her role of being Helen's friend and helper. At first everything worked out well. But as the years went by, John found it more and more difficult to live with two very famous and very busy women. In 1914 he moved out of the house, and though the three of them stayed friends, he never lived with his wife and Helen again.

When John Macy moved out, it was too much for Helen and Annie to manage on their own, so they hired Polly Thomson. Polly was a 24-year-old Scottish woman. She started out as Helen's housekeeper, but soon she became a very good friend and helper to both Helen and Annie.

The years sped by. Helen continued to write books and talk about the needs of the physically challenged.

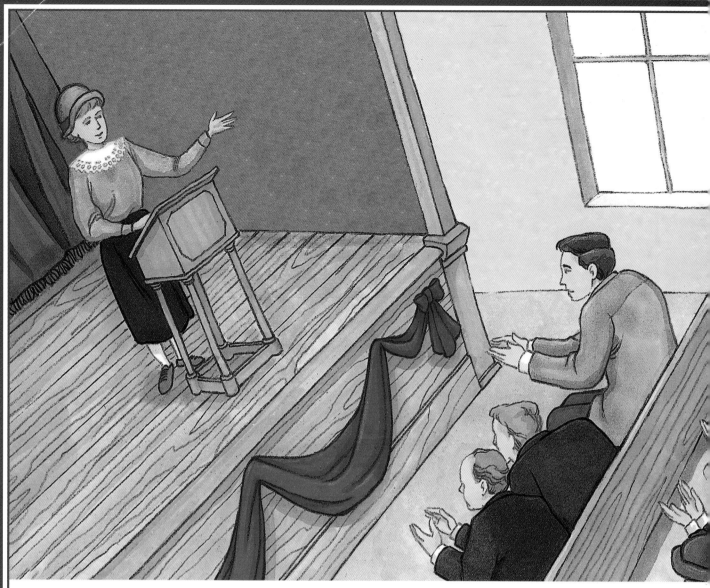

In 1924 Helen, Annie, and Polly set out together and travelled to more than 100 cities, speaking for the newly formed American Foundation for the Blind (AFB). On her travels, Helen met many blind children and was reminded how hard it was to learn five different raised dot alphabets. Now that she was famous, Helen could do something about the problem. She talked to many teachers of the blind and convinced them to use the same system. In 1932, European Braille was accepted as the world standard. Helen encouraged many wealthy people, such as John D. Rockefeller and Andrew Carnegie, to pay for hundreds of books to be translated into Braille. Now blind children all over the world

were able to read books just like sighted children.

In 1936, at the age of 70, Annie Sullivan died. Helen felt very alone. It had been nearly fifty years since their first meeting in Alabama. From that time on, they had spent nearly every day together, sharing their hopes and dreams. Later, Helen wrote about how she felt: "The light, the music, and the glory of life had been withdrawn."

Helen was discouraged at the loss of her partner, but she knew there was still more work for her to do. Polly Thomson took Annie's place as Helen's special helper, and together they travelled to 35 countries, speaking about how to help people with all kinds of physical challenges.

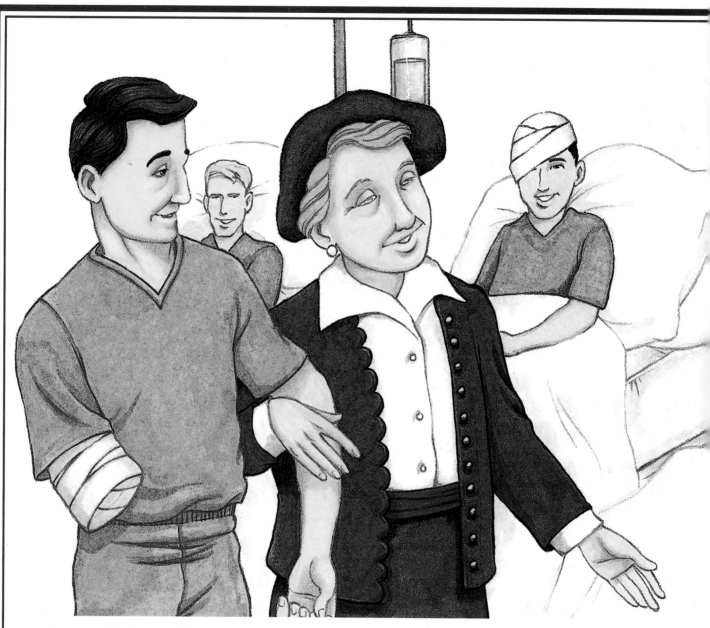

One of their favorite visits was to Japan where they met with the Emperor. While in Japan they raised enough money to build many schools for blind children.

Soon the Second World War began. Helen was very sad because Japan was now the enemy.

Thousands of American soldiers were badly injured in all the fighting—some lost arms or legs, others lost their hearing or sight. As they lay in military hospitals, many of them thought about all the things they could no longer do. What was the use of trying to get better?

President Roosevelt knew the men needed encourage-

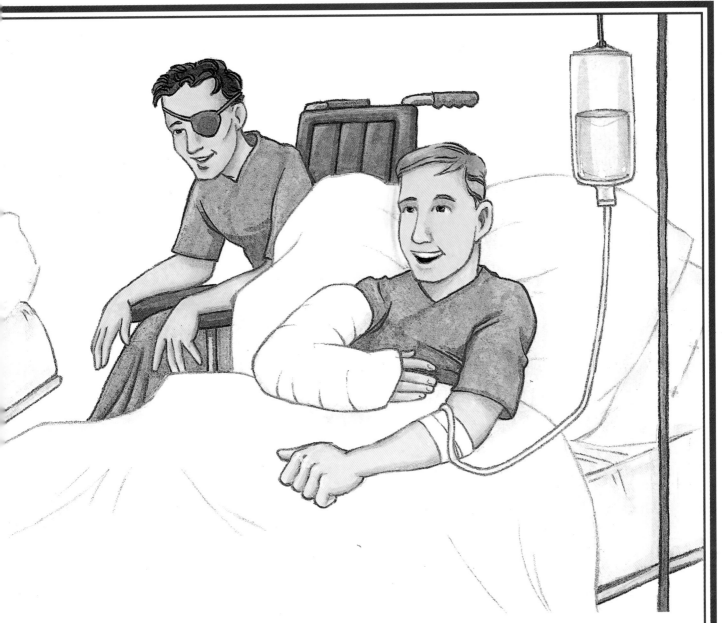

ment, so he asked Helen if she would visit them. Helen agreed and began a tour. Whenever she walked into a hospital room and smiled at a soldier, something wonderful happened. The soldier looked at the blind and deaf woman who had been all over the world helping others and thought, "If she can do it, I can, too." Later when they went home, hundreds of soldiers wrote to Helen, thanking her for reminding them of all the things they could still do. These wounded soldiers didn't know it, but Helen's visits helped her to keep on going, too. She called the visits the "crowning experience" of her life.

After the war, Helen and Polly travelled the world again, helping governments set up schools and libraries for blind children.

By now, Helen had written five books, but there was still one more she wanted to write—one to honor her teacher, Annie. She considered the day she met Annie as the most important day of her life. Helen said in a speech, "My birthday can never mean as much to me as the arrival of Annie Sullivan on March 3rd, 1887. That was my soul's birth day."

Helen spent several years writing the book about Annie, and when it was nearly finished she and Polly embarked on another overseas trip. While they were away in Rome, their house in Connecticut burned down. Everything Helen owned—including the nearly completed book—was destroyed. Helen was so disappointed, but she didn't let it get her down. When she got back, she started writing the book all over again. Finally, after twenty years of planning and writing, *Teacher: Anne Sullivan Macy* was published.

In 1961, Polly Thomson became very sick. Everyone could see she was going to die. Helen told a friend, "I can only pray that she may soon be among the friends awaiting me in Heaven, strong and full of joy in the beautiful work they have done on earth. It will be most lonely for me, but I shall rejoice in Polly's beautiful new life."

Before long, Helen had lost her second special friend. Helen was now 80 years old, and it was time to give up travelling and public speaking. She lived quietly at her new house in Connecticut. She had rails built all around the paths in her garden so she could walk alone in nature. Helen still loved the feel of the soft flower petals, the smell of the blossoms on the fruit trees, and the warmth of the sun on her face, just as she had all those years ago when she was a little girl in Alabama.

In 1968, just before her eighty-eighth birthday, Helen died peacefully at home. Radio and television around the world rushed to announce the sad news. When people heard of her death, they paused to remember her life. Presidents and kings sent flowers and special messages. Soldiers recalled her loving visits.

Blind and deaf children silently thanked her for their schools and Braille books. And all who knew her acknowledged her amazing courage.

In overcoming the difficulties that challenged her faith, Helen Keller turned the difficulties around. She brought inspiration to everyone by facing her challenges and then challenging the world.

Authors' Notes

Pages

5. Doctors today are reasonably sure that Helen had scarlet fever. Her doctor didn't know what it was, so he called it, "acute congestion of the stomach and brain." Scarlet fever can now be treated by penicillin.

6. Helen's father was called Captain Keller because he had been a Captain in the Confederate Army during the Civil War.

15. Laura Bridgman was 58 years old the first time Helen met her. She could read Braille and communicate with hand signs, but unlike Helen she did not like to be around people. Annie Sullivan spent a lot of time with her while she was a student at the Perkins Institute. From learning to communicate with Miss Bridgman, Annie knew how to help Helen.

16. Annie Sullivan went blind because of an eye disease which scratched the inside of her eyes. She had many operations over her lifetime to help the problem. Sometimes she was able to see quite well, and at other times, she was almost blind herself.

16. A poorhouse was a huge rooming house where people with no money or family could stay. The conditions were very bad, and many of the occupants were drunkards or insane.

21. For the rest of her life, Helen never called Annie any other name but "teacher".

26. Braille was invented by the Frenchman Louis Braille in 1826. A series of raised dots are used to show different letters of the alphabet. The blind people read these dots with their fingers.

30. Helen was very fond of dogs. She always owned at least one.

32. Tommy Stringer completed his education and went on to become a carpenter.

33. Captain Keller was not a good businessman and he was beginning to run out of money to help Helen. Alexander Graham Bell and some of his rich friends paid for this visit to Niagara Falls, and many of the other things that Helen and Annie needed.

34. Helen's father died when Helen was 15-years-old. Her mother died when Helen was 41-years-old.

46. Helen Keller's remains were placed next to those of her special helpers Annie Sullivan and Polly Thomson in Washington, D.C.'s National Cathedral.

DATE DUE

JAN 1 4 '03	JAN 18 '06	MAR 1 5 2016
FEB 10 '03	APR 16 04	JAN 1 8 2017
MAY 15 '03	JUN 1 1 07	5/26/17
NOV 12 '03	MAR 13 '08	JUN 0 5 2017
NON 19 03	MAR 1 9 08	4/20/18
JAN 1 4 '04	APR 08 08	
JAN 2 6 04	JUN 13 08	
FEB 2 '04	MAR 08 '11	
MAR 2 9 '04	APR 1 8 '10	
APR 5 '04		
MAY 3 '04	2/13/13	
OCT 16 04	MAR 2 0 2013	
MAR 1 7 05	OCT 2 4 2013	
MAR 21 '05	NOV 0 5 2015	
MAY 2 05	1/4/16	
MAY 1 8 05	2/8/16	
JAN 10 '06	6/7/16	

B
KELLER

Benge, Janet

HELEN KELLER FACING HER
     CHALLENGES CHALLENGING
THE WORLD